Gold Bar Bob Menendez Trial I

by Matthew Russell Lee

Inner City Press

May 13-June 13, 2024

TABLE OF CONTENTS

Chapter 1: From Union City to SDNY

Chapter 2: Daibes, Day Before Sickness

Chapter 3: US v Menendez Jury Selection May 14, 2024

Chapter 4: Car One and Two, Second Fiddle

Chapter 5: US v Menendez Jury Selection May 15, 2024

Chapter 6: The Selected Jurors

Chapter 7: Opening Arguments

Chapter 8: Menendez Trial Day May 21, 2024

Chapter 9: From Underdog to Gold Bar Bob

Chapter 10: Menendez Trial Day May 29, 2024

Chapter 11: Playing God in the SFRC

Chapter 12: Menendez Trial Day May 30, 2024

Chapter 13: Omega 7

Chapter 14: Menendez Trial Day May 31, 2024

Chapter 15: Short Eyes of Union City

Chapter 16: Menendez Trial Day June 5, 2024

Chapter 17: Uribe and Jersey All the Way Back

Chapter 18: Big Bob One and Two

Chapter 19: Menendez Trial Day June 6, 2024

Chapter 20: From Uribe to Grewal

Chapter 21: Menendez Trial Day June 7, 2024

Chapter 22: Voice of Uribe

Chapter 23: Menendez Trial Day June 10, 2024

Chapter 24: Beef Liver Strategy

Chapter 25: Menendez Trial Day June 11, 2024

Chapter 26: Strip Club and Short Eyes Out

Chapter 27: Menendez Trial Day June 12, 2024

Chapter 28: Full Circle, William Musto

Chapter 29: Menendez Trial Day Interruptus June 13, 2024

Chapter 1: From Union City to SDNY

Senator Bob Menendez of New Jersey pushed the Senate Foreign Relations Committee hard right on Cuba and Iran until he ran into an indictment for helping Egypt and Qatar. This is that story.

Menendez testified against his mentor William Musto, wearing a bullet-proof vest, and donated for the defense of anti-Castro bombers of Omega 7.

By 2024 he decried Jose Uribe who testified against him, after deploying the cards of terrorism, sexual harassment and nepotism against nominees.

He wanted his son Rob, who said he did not speak Spanish, to take his seat. He vowed to run as an independent. Outside the court he took Inner City Press' questions about what his wife Nadine had been texting thanks for.

Tomorrow you'll see the truth, he said. This is that tomorrow - and Fred Daibes feels sick.

Chapter 2: Daibes, Day Before Sickness

Every day I sit at the back table
Waiting for the toxic waste
And gold bar stories to begin
An eye on Al Jazeera
My old stomping ground

PCPs in Building 12
Spread 'em on a ballfield
Glass tower condos
For sale to Qatar princes

Or even Egyptian meat mafia
Met through my friend Will
Bob was the least of it
But here I am
Waiting for the gold bar to drop

Feeling sick

Chapter 3: Menendez Jury Selection May 14

Judge Sidney Stein: Prospective jurors, I'm going to ask you to come back tomorrow morning at 9:45 am, I have some questions the whole group

May 14: Juror 42, I'm single. I have two sons, one is a bartender in Miami. My other son is in maintenance.
Judge: Level of education?
42: High school
Judge: Ma'am, we'll end with you.
Juror 40: I have a masters in library science. NYT, WaPo, WNYC. Social media, Instagram

Judge Stein: Once I finish this round [tomorrow] lawyers will use their peremptories and we should have a jury by the end of the morning.

Judge Stein has come back, after the prospective jurors have left.
Judge Stein: If all goes well, we'll have

openings tomorrow. So you are entitled to my rulings. I am precluding Doctor Rosenbaum. It just doesn't stand up. The CPA? He can testify under strictures

Judge Stein: He can testify to Senator Menendez' known inflows and outflows. He's a CPA. The other expert on Egypt, he can speak about Sisi and the Muslim Brotherhood. And Morsi. But we're not going back to the Pharaohs. And nothing about the halal contract

Judge Stein: I'm going to file an opinion tomorrow denying Mr. Menendez' request for subpoenas under Rule 15. See you tomorrow.

Chapter 4: Car One and Two, Second Fiddle

Those red hatted freaks
Cheering at Trump's motorcade
Then spitting at my Honda
And calling me a pedo

It's been weeks
It's been hell.
No Nadine in court
My sad text messages
On the screen for all to see.

Now after the conviction next door
My exits more easy
Does no one care
About my crucifixion?

Car 2

When I go out to the car
Fancier this time
The lady from Univision
Asked me how I feel
Like she did in Union City
Arroz y habichuelas
I shall return
Volere

Chapter 5: Jury Selection May 15, 2024

....Prospective juror 61: I studied in Bronx Community College to be electrician, now I care for my mother.
Judge Stein: You live with a spouse? A wife?
61: I am divorced. My girlfriend is personal assistant too. My mother is 80-more year old. Juanito Peralta, 61

Good morning! I'm Senator 63. I mean, Juror 63. I live in Harlem New York, work on brands. I get Apple News. I design different things, I'm a saxophonist
Judge Stein: We lost one of the saxophone tribe the other day.
63: Sorry.
Judge: David Sanborn

Juror 93, Westchester with my wife, who works at a non-profit in Queens. I'm the pastor in a church and listen to Al Jazeera, WBAI, Haaretz [Others said Axios & cosplay]

Judge Stein: A dual masters?
93: Divinity and theology. I love long walks in the park

Juror 88: Upper West Side Harlem. I am a custodian at Queens Library. TikTok, YouTube. Hobbies? Video games, telling my girlfriend the Knicks are going to win the championship.
Juror 100: Degree in Black Studies. I am a self-employed business consultant

Next prospect: Podcasts? I listen to Sean Hannity, Mark Levin. I read the Epoch Times.
Next: I work at JFK, I have an Instagram, I consider myself a sports junkie, I like to brew beer and drink it.
Judge: What does your wife do? A: Stay at home Mom.

Next prosect: I use Mastodon. I play the drums.
Judge: What does your wife do? A: Artist, for herself, sells it on Instagram.
111: An MFA in music, I work for a firm active in Broadway shows. Gothamist. I'm on

Facebook and sometimes Threads. Pod Save America.

Prosecutors and defense lawyers are off with Judge Stein.
Menendez is sitting alone at the front defense table; co-defendants at table further back.
We'll have results of jury selection - and then openings
Watch this feed

All rise!
Judge Stein: Now the lawyers will exercise their peremptory challenges. The lawyers will go back into the jury deliberation room. We should be back in 10 or 15 min [then later today, opening arguments. And *maybe* some from the robing/deliberations room

All rise!
Judge Stein: Please be seated. Will the following jurors please take their seats, in order
[Some numbers read out]
Judge: No, that's an error. [Starts over; most sent back down]. Now you will be sworn, so

help you God. Let me tell you about your duty

Judge Stein: The defendants - you must look at each one separately, there's no grouping here - are presumed innocent. You are the deciders of the facts. We will take a lunch break, then the first opening statement, by the government - that's set by law

Judge Stein: Don't eat in the cafeteria - the good is adequate, but you are not missing anything. I eat in the cafeteria most days, just to save time. Don't greet the lawyers - if you nod because you recognize someone, that's understandable.

Judge Stein: OK, you may go out for lunch. I'll give you more time today - we'll see you at 2:25 for opening statements.
[Jurors leave]
Judge Stein: Let's talk about the slides

Judge Stein: Much of this sounds like a campaign...
Menendez's lawyer: We will be putting on witnesses about this.

Assistant US Attorney: He wants to put in the names of his two children.
Judge Stein: Strike their names. But the rest is in.

Judge Stein: What is 4?
Menendez' lawyer: It was an instruction to Sen Menendez how to disclose the gold bars- he was told to delete the word "parental gift."
AUSA Richenthal: We won't bring it in as hearsay
Menendez lawyer: It's for state of mind
Judge: Stricken

Judge Stein: The MLK on We are not makers of history - why?
Menendez's lawyer: It's relevant to our generational trauma argument.
AUSA: Doctor King was not speaking about Senator Menendez, or cash, or gold.
Judge Stein: Some pablum is OK

Judge Stein: I agree, it's too general. I'm going to strike it, with my apologies to Doctor King and General Powell.
Menendez's lawyer: May I express the quote without attribution?

Judge Stein: I'll allow it. But I'm striking Number 7.

Menendez's lawyer: This is the Senator's letter to AG Holder, to show he did it before -
AUSA: It's meant to engender sympathy.
Judge Stein: It's out.
Menendez's lawyer: The next is about the Qatar [pronounces it Cutter] evidence

Judge: What is a voice vote?
Menendez's lawyer: There was only one voice.
AUSA: We allege Mr. Menendez accepted those things for greed, he understood it was Mr. Daibes understanding that the government of Qatar was to be benefited.

Judge Stein: Reporting out of Committee is important - I know, from nominated judges getting reported out of Judiciary. So - let me read it again.
Menendez's lawyer: It was a voice vote.
Judge Stein: You're asking the jury to infer he had nothing to do with S.Res 390

AUSA Richenthal: Because of the Constitution we are not going to argue, about the Senate Resolution, that he did anything wrong. But if they say he did nothing on it, we have a right to respond.

Judge Stein: He was the chair. Now, Secretary Blinken, Slide 12?

Menendez's lawyer: Blinken did the same thing, falling all over himself to praise Qatar.
Judge: Say it, but slide is out. See you 2:20

Chapter 6: The Selected Jurors

Seat 1 - Juror 6. Seat 2 - Juror 9. Seat 3 - Juror 12. Seat 4 - Juror 17. Seat 5 - Juror 21. Seat 6 - Juror 22. And so forth. And them the timing:

Pomerantz 45 minutes

Weitzman 60 minutes

Lustberg 30 minutes

Chapter 7: Opening Arguments, May 15, 2024

Judge Stein: Ms. Pomerantz?
AUSA Pomerantz: This case is about a public official who put need first. He put his own interest before the people. He put his power up for sale. This is Robert Menendez, Senator of NJ

AUSA: He sold his power for gold, to Hana. But that's not all the bribes he took - he also took from NJ real estate development Daibes. He also gave gold bars, and cash in envelopes. The FBI found gold and $400,000 in cash, in shoes and jackets

AUSA: The defendant gave Egypt non-public US government information. In exchange for a Mercedes he promised to try to disrupt a criminal case against two associates of Hana. And he promised to try to influence a Federal criminal case against Daibes

AUSA: This was political for profit. This is what this trial is all about. Menendez used his wife as a go-between. She communicated with the bribed payers, and collected some. It started with Menendez planning to help Hana and the government of Egypt

AUSA: Menendez was chair of the Senate Foreign Relations Committee. He could hold up billions. He dated Nadine, married her. She was friends with Hana. Hana was a failed businessman but he believed if he bribed for Egypt he'd be helped

AUSA: Egyptian officials asked Menendez to help Egypt. He passed on non-public information about the US Embassy in Egypt to the government there. He ghostwrote a letter about Egypt's human rights record and abuses, to get money unfrozen. He greenlighted weapons

AUSA: So then Hana got a business monopoly from the Egyptian government, the only company approving shipments of US beef to Egypt. He had no experience, but he had a US Senator in his pocket, arranging military aid. He paid Nadine, but US companies were cut out

AUSA: The USDA contacted Egypt and protested, saying US companies were being hurt. Hana heard, and ran to Menendez. So Menendez called a high-level official at the USDA and said, Stop opposing the monopoly. They set up Strategic Int'l Business Consultants

AUSA: It was a bribe collecting company; it had only Nadine. She demanded to get paid - her mortgage payments. But Hana was slow. So Nadine went to Daibes - and then Hana paid. Daibes stayed involved - he handed a bribe to Menendez, a check from Hana

AUSA: It was quid pro quo, this for that. Sham paychecks and gold from Hana for Menendez' promises of military aid to Egypt. That's only the first part. Hana was also working with insurer Jose Uribe to give a Mercedes to Bob and Nadine

AUSA: A trucker was being investigated in NJ for insurance fraud. But Menendez could disrupt it - because Nadine needed a car, a brand-new Mercedes convertible.

[Note: Menendez these days is leaving SDNY in a Honda with FOP plates:

AUSA: Nadine got $15,000 cash in a parking lot, made a down payment on the Mercedes. She wrote to Menendez, WE now own a 2019 Mercedes. And Uribe made the payments. He went to Menendez directly - Menendez met the NJ AG and complained

AUSA: When the US Attorney for NJ was resigning, Menendez tried to get a new one to help Daibes. He interviewed the candidate and only brought up Daibes, he said he hoped the candidate would look into Daibes case is he became US Attorney.

AUSA: But the candidate said he might have to recuse himself from Daibes case. So Menendez put forward a second candidate - but it fell through. Back to the first candidate - he got in, and was recused. Menendez still tried to get him involved.

AUSA: The gold bars were each worth $50,000. Menendez kept Googling the price of a kilo of gold. Daibes also gave cash - it was found in Menendez's home, with Daibes'

DNA on it. Then there was Qatar. Daibes bribed Menendez to help Qatar, get it praised in Congress

AUSA: Daibes wanted a Qatari investment in his business, in exchange for getting Qatar praised in the US Congress. Bob and Nadine tried to cover up. Menendez and Daibes are both charged with obstruction of justice. You are going to see the gold

AUSA: Each gold bar in the Menendez home was a unique serial number - which tracked back to Hana and Daibes. We'll take you back into the scheme, minute by minute. You'll see Daibes text Menendez a picture of a gold bar. Menendez used Nadine to send texts

AUSA: You're going to hear from officials Menendez promised to influence - the USDA official, the NJ AG, and the US Attorney for NJ. Each will tell you what Menendez said to them. They didn't know why. You will hear from Jose Uribe

AUSA: Uribe will describe his conversations with all of them. He pled guilty to bribing Menendez and other crimes. He has a

cooperation agreement. Use your common sense. You will find that these defendants are guilty.
Judge Stein: Mr. Weitzman?

Menendez's lawyer Avi Weitzman: Senator Menendez is a patriot. Bob, as he is known to his friends and family, started off running for Union City Board of Ed. After that he became Mayor of Union City. Then state legislature -- 33 years ago, to Congress.

Menendez's lawyer: His family lost everything when they left Cuba. He was first person in his family to go to college, then law school at Rutgers. He wasn't looking for a payday.
Judge Stein: This is what you believe the evidence will show? Please make that clear

Menendez's lawyer: Bob has fought for health care, equity... He's the proud father of two children. He could have made more money elsewhere
Judge Stein: Apparently, that's what the evidence is going to show. Jurors, this is not about whether the lawyer believes it

Menendez' lawyer: There will be no witness who says they ever discussed a bribe with Senator Menendez. Not one email or 1 text by Senator Menendez. They searched every iCloud, every outhouse-
AUSA: Objection!
Judge Stein: Sustained. The actions of US not at issue

Menendez's lawyer: Bob was doing his job. He complained of discrimination and reached out. He engaged in diplomacy. The case rests on speculation, not actual bribes. There's an elephant in the room, a green and gold elephant. Smells weird? Resist that

Menendez's lawyer: You will conclude the government has not met its burden. The gold bars? Where were they? In a closet that was a locked closet - NADINE's closet, filled with her clothes. The Senator did not know the gold bars were there

Menendez's lawyer: Bob knew Nadine had FAMILY gold. Me, I'm an identical twin. I-
AUSA: Objection!
Judge Stein: Sustained. Stick to the evidence.

And, I never knew you were a twin.
Menendez's lawyer: Back to Bob and Nadine. Bob was married 29 years then divorced

Menendez' lawyer: Bob met Nadine, she is a tall and beautiful global woman who grew up in Lebanon and calls him Amour de ma vie, love of my life. From dating in 2018 to April 2020, they lived apart. Bob lived in DC, paid $1600 a month, and an apartment in NJ.

Menendez' lawyer: Bob moved into Nadine's home; they had separate finances. They had a separate cell phone plan. So he didn't know about the gold bars. Nadine had financial concerns that she kept from Bob. She was supported by a former husband

Menendez' lawyer: Nadine didn't let Bob know who she was asking for money from. She asked Hana and Daibes and Uribe. She kept Bob sidelined. Nadine had these relationships long before she met Bob. Sure she got gold from her friends. But what did Bob know?

Menendez' lawyer: Do you remember the game, Where's Waldo?

AUSA: Objection!

Menendez's lawyer: I gave them the slide, your Honor. They didn't object.

It's in.

Menendez's lawyer: Where's Bob? Doing his job.

Menendez's lawyer: Bob searched for gold prices because Nadine's family has long owed gold. In Lebanon they collect gold. Local currencies can be unstable. Nadine subsisted on the gold bars. Some people are not great at saving

Menendez's lawyer: Nadine wanted to pay off her mortgage with gold. Bob thought the gold was from her family. When you're a sitting Senator you need to made disclosures. He asked Nadine for info and reported it. He was not told everything

Menendez' lawyer: He disclosed gold bars, before he ever learned of any FBI investigation. This proves he didn't receive bribes. The cash? He moved in with a lot of cash. Bags of cash which he stores in the basement. He stored them in his boots.

Menendez' lawyer: A famous man once said, We are not makers of history [MLK] I'm the grandson of Holocaust survivors-

Judge Stein: Sustained! This case is not about you!

Menendez's lawyer: It's not always rational. Sen Menendez, his family lost everything but cash

Menendez's lawyer: Here's a $100 bill with a series 2006. They have long been stored. What about the fingerprints and DNA? None on the Senator's cash. Daibes prints are on his wife's closet. Let's look at the master bedroom

Menendez' lawyer: One envelope in the basement had Daibes' fingerprints. Not surprising. They have been friendly for 30 years. It's just an envelope. Nadine's closet? Keep an open mind. Constituent services.

Menendez's lawyer: He's permitted to provide constituent services for friends - because listening to a friend is not a crime. Not everything a Senator does is an official act.

We'll talk about Jose Uribe's lies. But he never discussed bribes with Bob.

Menendez's lawyer: Uribe, it was about Latino truckers being targeted. The indictment is just words-
AUSA: Objection!
Judge Stein: Sustained. It was voted on by a grand jury.
Menendez's lawyer: Bob was engaged in diplomacy. The US supports Egypt. Bob was nuanced

Menendez's lawyer: Bob wrote to Mike Pompeo about rights in Egypt. He met the President of Egypt and took him to task, monitored by the ambassador. Arms sales to Egypt are wanted, requested and approved. Senator Menendez had no magic wand.

Menendez's lawyer: Bob was doing diplomacy, carrot and stick. He was doing a diplomacy dance with a dictator. On the halal, there was a two-to-four-minute call, no pressure. Bob was doing his job, he was doing his job the right way.

Menendez' lawyer: A Senator is allowed to complain to a Federal agency - even allowed to yell. It's not illegal. It's Constitutionally protected. Lots of people have consulting companies. Bob and Nadine were dating- Bob wasn't even in the house

Menendez' lawyer: If the payments were bribes, why were they stopped after three months?
AUSA: Objection!
Judge Stein: I'll allow it. It's speculation, but based off the evidence.
Menendez' lawyer: Bob advocates for the disadvantaged.
Judge: Don't sermonize

Menendez's lawyer: Latino truckers were being discriminated against by the NJ AG [now SEC Enforcement official - apparently he'll testify in US v. Menendez] - the Senator looked into it. Bob was doing his job. The Government is unfairly twisting

Menendez' lawyer: The Mercedes was not a bribe to Bob. Nadine had a Mercedes and got into a crash. She got a new one, just one year into their dating. Nadine's family was in the Persian carpet business. Bob told Nadine to pay it back, not to obstruct.

Menendez' lawyer: Bob's nomination of Phil Sellinger was not based on a bribe. He wasn't Bob's first choice - he preferred Esther Suarez but she was a lightning rod. Bob thought Sellinger was biased against Daibes, didn't want it to upend the nomination

Menendez' lawyer: When Sellinger was removed from Daibes' case, he was replaced by Vikas Khanna, relative of the Congressman from California. Bob didn't raise Daibes to him. Daibes had a project in Edgewater, four beautiful towers - Bob knew Heritage Advisors

Menendez's lawyers: Heritage Advisers is for a member of Qatar's royal family, but not Qatar, they won't prove it. It wanted in on this investment on the New Jersey waterfront. And in the Senate, praise for Qatar. You'll see others praising them- the Sect of State

Menendez's lawyer: There thousands of al Thanis. Thousands and thousands!

Judge Stein: How much longer do you have?
Menendez's lawyer: One page. Ask yourself, Where's Bob? Where's Bob? You have a man's life time of public service in your hands

Menendez's lawyer: Consider the evidence. Thank you.
Judge Stein: I'll give you a break

But when Judge Stein returns he says: My deputy informs me some jurors cannot stay past 5 pm. So we will let you go now. Jurors leave.
Defense counsel: Ms. Pomerantz's opening violated the Speech and Debate Clause instruction...She said he was going to sign off

Defense: That merits a mistrial. Oh and I have a second point. Ms. Pomerantz said Mr. Daibes was looking for an investment from Qatar... "Like by supporting a Senate resolution praising Qatar" - Mr. Richenthal said the government was not going to do this

Judge Stein: It's true you were not supposed to say "praising Qatar."
AUSA Richenthal: Accepting payment is not a legislative act.
Defense: This is angels dancing on the head of a pin. We think they'll be a righteous outcome here, but on appeal...

Defense: Only lawyers could come up with this theory
Judge Stein: With Speech and Debate, the issue is what is a legislative act, it's not here. Motion for mistrial denied. Government, watch the line on the Qatar resolution.

Menendez's lawyer Fee: Ms. Pomerantz said Menendez helped Egypt
Judge Stein: That's fine.
Fee: It's not. The line is untenable. A promise doesn't help Egypt.
AUSA: Of course it helps Egypt to give them an inside track, inside information

Judge Stein: Mr. Richenthal has the better part of the argument. We're far away from core Speech and Debate.
Fee: Speech and Debate cannot be construed

narrowly. This is so narrow you can barely see it from the side. They are making a hyper technical argument

Judge Stein: Motion for mistrial denied. Adjourned.

Chapter 8: Menendez Trial Day May 16, 2024

OK - now US v Menendez, agent on the stand testifying to finding gold bars, and how his fingerprints got on a bag. Inner City Press, covering the case, aims to upload as many of these gold bar exhibits as possible. Testimony ongoing for now, thread below

Menendez' lawyer: Are you aware that none of Bob Menendez' prints were found on that bag?
Agent: No.
Menendez's lawyer: Did you know whose home that was?
Agent: I thought it was Bob Menendez' home. My task was to search it

Judge Stein: How much more cross do you have?
Menendez' lawyer: Thirty minutes or so.
Judge Stein: We'll start tomorrow at 10 am

May 17

OK - US v. Menendez resumes with cross examination about gold bars and cash found during the search. Inner City Press is covering the case and will live tweet, thread below

Judge Stein: Mr. Fee, how much more cross do you have?
Menendez's lawyer Fee: 45 minutes. Agent, I'm going to show you some of the walk-through video. We offer it into evidence.
Assistant US Attorney: No objection.
Judge Stein: Admitted.

[Video is shown of master bedroom, exercise machine, bathroom - then closet.]
Menendez' lawyer Fee: Agent, that's the closet that had been locked, in Room Charlie?
Agent: Yes.
[Video stops and shows framed currency on the wall]
Fee: You see the Senator's blazer?

Agent: Yes, the blazer was in Room Bravo, not Room Charlie.
Menendez's lawyer Fee: So yesterday's testimony was incorrect?
Agent: Today's testimony is true.
Fee: What about this tie with rodents and

cheese and skulls - is that the only male article of clothing?

Agent: I don't think I can make that determination.

Menendez's lawyer Fee: Anything male in this photo of Nadine's closet?

Agent: I can't see what is behind the dresses. I did not search this closet.

Fee: There was no response at Nadine's house?

Agent: Yes.

Menendez's lawyer Fee: You put tape over the camera and turned off the wi-fi -- why?

Agent: So no one could wipe the computer, or see where we were in the house.

Fee: So only the FBI was able to record what the FBI did?

AUSA: Objection!

Judge Stein: Sustained

Menendez' lawyer Fee: Today, you could use body cameras for this?

Agent: We didn't have the cameras back then.

Fee: You put the tape over the Ring and entered through the garage - you had the code from Senator Menendez?

Agent: I got it from a case agent

Re-direct

Assistant US Attorney: Where did the FBI find the cash, in the jacket?

Agent: In Room U.

AUSA: This yellow bag, who far was it from the jacket marked with the Post-It [TM] notes?

Agent: Inches.

AUSA: No further questions

Judge Stein: Next witness

James Tate, I am an Agricultural Attache at the US Embassy in Santiago de Chile.

AUSA: Who do you work for?

Witness: USDA, I'm a career foreign services officer for USDA. I went to Texas A&M. I previously served in Cairo, Egypt for four years, from 2015 to 2019

AUSA: Is who works in the US Embassy public information?

Tate: Absolutely not. It is sensitive. People can be targeted. There, I covered Egypt, Israel and Lebanon.... In many countries, dissidents of the government are targeted by the government

AUSA: Did you find that the government of Egypt targeted dissidents?
Witness: Yes.
AUSA: What is the role of USDA in the export of meat?
Witness: An expert must attest to wholesomeness - it's 9060-5
Judge Stein: Slow down. This is new to all of us.

Tate: Egypt imports 70% of the US' beef liver. With green peppers, if you're in Cairo, recommend it. (Chuckles). Also, it's affordable.
AUSA: Did Egypt require halal certification?
Tate: Yes.
AUSA: Did Egypt have requirements about who could certify?
A: Yes.

Tate: It was changed to a single certifier.
AUSA: What is that called?
Tate: A monopoly. It was given to ISEG

Halal. It is owned by Wael Hana, sometimes called Will Hana

AUSA: I have (much) more with this witness, is this a good time to break?

USDA's Tate: The Undersecretary and I had expected a meeting with the Egyptian government - but their minister brought Mr. Hana with them. We explained if her remained, we could not be as candid.
AUSA: Then what?
Tate: Their minister spoke to Hana. He was upset

AUSA: Show the witness 8b-48. What is this?
Tate: Photo of the meeting.
Judge Stein: Is that an Egyptian flag next to the American flag?
Tate: It is. After the meeting ended, we had a Halal certifiers meeting at the hotel in Arlington, the Crystal City Marriott.

Tate: There was Halal Co from the Atlanta area, the Hana's firm and two others.
AUSA: Did you use email? Show the witness 8b-1 and 2
[Menendez is slumped back in his chair at defense table, his head resting on / in his left hand]

AUSA: Did the Egyptian official come to here the other applicants?
Tate: No. I found him down in the restaurant having lunch with Mr. Hana.
AUSA: What did you do?
Tate: He was an hour late, I asked him to come. He said, Don't worry. The deputy minister glared at me

AUSA: Show the exhibit - what was your role?
[Letter to Egypt's deputy minister Dr. Mona Mehrev, the glarer]
Tate: I drafted it. We understood that their move to monopoly would have a negative impact on US businesses.

Judge Stein: Let's break here.

Chapter 9: Trial Day May 21, 2024

OK - now US v. Menendez, witness on stand testifying on direct about "loans" to Nadine Menendez and her "consulting' contracts - Inner City Press is covering the case in all ways and will live tweet, thread below

Assistant US Attorney: The contract with Mrs. Menendez' firm, how much was it for?
Witness: $10,000 a month, until someone canceled it.
Cross by Hana's lawyer
Hana's lawyer: You wrote to Nadine, no interest loan that he [Wael Hana] authorized?
Witness: I did

Hana's lawyer: Mr. Hana's daily calls with Egypt, you have no idea if they were about operational issues like shipping, do you?
AUSA: Objection!
Judge Sidney Stein: Sustained. Does he know the topic of the calls.
Witness: I don't.

Bob Menendez's lawyer: You understood Nadine needed help with a mortgage, and Mr. Hana told you he wanted to help, that she was like a sister to him?
Witness: I don't remember him saying that. But he wanted to give her a loan... I met her in a restaurant

Bob Menendez's lawyer: You were impressed by her?
Witness: She's an impressive lady. She was well dressed and had an expensive watch on, which I took to mean success.
Bob Menendez' lawyer: Did she name drop?
Witness: Yes. I don't remember what names she dropped

Bob Menendez's lawyer: Did she mention the Real Housewives - but not Senator Menendez?
Witness: She did not mention Senator Menendez. She was offended that Will had me, a lawyer, draft a promissory note

Fred Daibes' lawyer: How old are you again?
Witness: 37.
Fred Daibes' lawyer: Are you aware Mr.

Daibes has adult children?
Witness: Which Mr. Daibes?
Fred Daibes' lawyer: Fred. Or Freddie as they call him in Edgewater: is he down to earth?
Witness: Yes.

Fred Daibes' lawyer: Have you lived in one of Mr. Daibes' buildings?
AUSA: Objection!
Judge Stein: I'll allow it.
Witness: Yes. Most beautiful building I have ever seen.
Fred Daibes' lawyer: In the office building, did return from the bathroom require a fob?
Yes

Judge Stein: Jurors, we've been at it for about two hours. Let's take a break.

They've back.
Judge Stein: Government, call your next witness.
AUSA: Joshua Paul - where did you previously work?
Paul (with British accent) The US State Department, Bureau of Political and Military

Affairs - America's defense diplomacy: armed transfers

Paul: I was responsible for the Bureau's relations with Congress, the media and civil society.
AUSA: You covered arms transfers?
Paul: Extensively so. Security assistance and weapons transfers, we have to notify Congress, and get funding.

Paul: We do about 300 arms transfers a year.
AUSA: Are you aware of a Senator named Robert Menendez?
Paul: Yes. He was on the Senate Foreign Relations Committee, the SFRC.
AUSA: How do holds work?
Paul: Within the 15 days, the chair or ranking member can put 1 on

AUSA: Where does the money go once appropriated?
Paul: For Egypt, as for Israel, it goes into an interest-bearing account in the Federal Reserve Bank of New York. For Egypt, some $90 million requires certification as to release of political prisoners

AUSA: How does a hold end?

Paul: The member lifts the hold, or the two years expire.

AUSA: How long is the review process for arms transfers to Egypt?

Paul: 40 days - it's in the slowest tier, Tier 3. Arms transfers to the Middle East are the most controversial

Judge Stein: We'll break here. I'd ask those in the courtroom to wait until the jurors have gone down in the elevators

Chapter 9: From Underdog to Gold Bar Bob

Kurt Wheelock had, almost despite himself, begun to see Menendez as a sort of underdog, twice prosecuted by the Fed, dumped or duped by his new wife, filmed stuffing his face with French fries on the morning of jury selection.

But. But.

Kurt went back and watched YouTube after YouTube of Menendez pontificating on the Senate Foreign Relations. He accused Kelly Craft of conflicts of interest, given her husband's business - this while Nadine was demanding a Mercedes and carpet fixing in exchange for favors he would do, from halal meat to insurance fraud cover-up.

He attached a nominee for not being up to "United Nations standards" - including Linda Thomson-Greenfield, for having given a speech at or for a CCP Confucius Institute event at a HBCU in Georgia.

Menendez had mocked a man from the San Diego Union-Tribune for sexual harassment, after having partied with Susan Rice about Sudan (while preparing to sell out to the military leader of next-door Egypt, and leak them State Department info).

Perhaps this level of hypocrisy was itself pitiable. Kurt would come back in the next day and continue to cover Menendez's (second) trial.

Chapter 10: Trial Day May 29, 2024

OK - now US v. Menendez, Special Agent on the stand putting in Egypt bribe evidence between Wael Hana and Nadine

Assistant US Attorney: Agent, please read what Nadine wrote to Senator Menendez.
Agent: He has not arrived yet at the Washington airport. He is coming with Sisi from Guyana.
AUSA: What was the name of the president of Egypt in 2019?
Agent: Sisi.

AUSA: Who's the sender here?
Agent: Wael Hana. To HHHH.
AUSA: Exhibit C-417, an email.
Agent: April 17, 2019 from W. Hana to HH number Gmail
"Please consider this email as a point-by-point response to Doctor Abdi. May I suggest that the response be as follows

Agent (reading) It is the government of Egypt, not the USDA, which decides on halal status. The personnel of the company are well versed in halal...
AUSA: Let's go to the timeline, GX 1302
Agent: Bertsch writes to other in USDA about decertification of others

AUSA: What's this?
Agent: Charge d'affaires to others, about the decertification and asking that the other companies be allowed to continue until this matter is resolved
AUSA: Page 49. Line 639, on May 3, 2019, what does HHHH sent to Hana?
Agent: OK to Hana's ISEG

AUSA: What does Nadine text to [Bob] Menendez?
Agent: That He is still mad at Will for talking about Halal
AUSA: Whose search history is this?
Agent: Robert Menendez. He's searching for April Corley

AUSA: What does Nadine text Menendez?
Agent: That protocol meeting is 15 minutes and that Will should respect that.
AUSA: And what did Menendez reply?
Agent: "Good for him."

AUSA: What does Nadine text Menendez?
Agent: Mon amour, to you want me to text or email you the info?
AUSA: What does Menendez do?
Agent: He calls Nadine for 6 minutes & 8 seconds.
AUSA: What does Hana do?
Agent: He send Nadine a link and she sends it to Menendez

AUSA: What is being sent here?
Agent: Names and salary levels, and job descriptions. Nadine is listed at $120,000.
AUSA: How much is that a month?
Menendez' lawyer: Objection!
Judge: Sustained

AUSA: What does this say?
Agent: April Corley will not accept your offer of $2 million. But she will accept $13.5 million

AUSA: What that the woman Senator Menendez Googled?
Menendez' lawyer: Objection! Leading!
Judge: Sustained.

AUSA: What does this say?
Agent: Although we accept that we are dealing with a private entity, we maintain this liability is that of Egypt and Egypt alone.
AUSA: And this?
Agent: "If the guy takes care of this with [Senator-1] he'll be set."

Judge Stein: Let's break here.

Back in US v. Menendez:
On the screen, Fred [Daibes] texts Nadine, "Nadine, I personally gave Bob a check for September... Please give me a rundown of what you believe you are owed."
AUSA: Then what does Nadine send?
Agent: Image files, to Fred Daibes.

Judge Stein: We are done for the day.

Chapter 11: Playing God in the SFRC

The Bozos the Orange Man
Brought before me
Lambs to the slaughter
In my SFRC

Kelly Krat, coal wife, playing hooky
The man from San Diego with the MeToo
And lack of preparation
Calling a nation a protectorate

Like a God I swatted them
Down and showed Nadine the video
As if she cared
Beef liver fingerprints
In her box

I got along with Susan Rice
I rehabilitated LTG
From the Confucius Institute
Nothing I couldn't do
Until I couldn't

Chapter 12: Trial Day May 30, 2024

Menendez' lawyer: Agent, how long have you been with the C-14 unit [of the FBI]?
Agent: Only about 3 months.
Menendez' lawyer: Yet you've been on the stand for days - you deserve battle pay
AUSA: Objection!
Judge Stein: Sustained. Counsel, you know better

Menendez' lawyer: You reviewed each document before they showed you the summary chart?
Agent: I took a holistic view.
Menendez' lawyer: Did the AUSA instruct you to generally familiarize yourself with the documents? Let me show you 3507-002.
Judge: To refresh you

Menendez's lawyer: Did you review documents beyond the ones included in the current chart?

Agent: Edit were made.

[For those following both, this is like Michael Cohen's texts about the 14-year-old crank caller, that he called Trump's bodyguard about]

Menendez's lawyer: Didn't you cut out this message by Senator Menendez, I don't want to interfere with your boyfriend?
Agent: It's not in the chart.
Menendez's lawyer: Do you know that Nadine had a boyfriend named Doug Anton?
AUSA: Objection!
Judge: Sustained

Menendez's lawyer: You are aware that are thousands of called between Nadine and Bob Menendez, but only a few are in your chart?
Agent: I imagine there are more.
Menendez's lawyer: Are you married sir and your wife sometimes uses your phone?
Objection! Sustained

Menendez's lawyer: Do you see Nadine's text to Bob, "I am at Mercedes, pray for me"? And Bob asks, What's wrong?

Agent: I see it.

Menendez's lawyer: And she didn't answer, and you don't know what was wrong, do you?

Agent: I don't.

Menendez's lawyer: Are you aware the "Oui mon amour" is "Yes my love"?

AUSA: Objection!

Judge: Sustained.

Menendez's lawyer: She says, "No bad test results" - do you know what that's about?

AUSA: Objection!

Judge: Sustained.

Menendez's lawyer: Let's talk about the NordicTrack, Nadine said it cost her $1600?

AUSA: Rule of completeness!

Menendez's lawyer: Is there any other record that shows Nadine told Senator Menendez that [Hana's] ISEG paid for the NordicTrack or Bow-Flex?

Not aware

Judge Stein: How much do you have left?

Menendez' lawyer: I'm a third of the way through.

Judge: It's been an hour

Menendez' lawyer: He testified for three days.

Judge: OK, let's continue

[Now Judge excuses the jury. Then:]

Judge: I've been giving you leeway. But you can't keep asking him to interpret these charts.

Menendez's lawyer: This is unfair.

AUSA: If you want to ask about Morton's Steakhouse's phone number and a Google search, fine

Judge Stein: You'll have to tie it to the chart. We are adjourned.

Chapter 13: Omega 7

I saw we fled Fidel
But we really fled Bastita
Monzon told me back then
If you want to rise you must

So I turned on my mentor
When I give money to Omega 7
I really believed in it
Or did I?

I drank cognac with Gwendolyn Beck
She of Epstein's black book or was it Giuffre
It's had to keep up with them
Hard and sharp, I wael survive
This Will Hana
His beef liver was a trap
They think they have me
But no one does.

Chapter 14: Trial Day May 31, 2024

OK - now US v. Sen Bob Menendez, Inner City Press is covering the trial (e.g., "Nadine Texts About Sisi Shown While Gold Bar Bob Steak at Morton's"

All rise!
Judge: Mr. Lustberg [counsel to Wael Hana] you may proceed.
Lustberg: You see this receipt, payment for the exercise machine?
Witness: Yes, a Paypal receipt.

Lustberg: Do you see this message in which Nadine Menendez calls Mr. Hana a brother?
Agent: I see it.
Lustberg: She wanted him to pay off her mortgage, correct?
Agent: I recall that generally.
Lustberg: Here she is asking for a wire
AUSA: Objection!
Sustained

Lustberg: This message from Jose Uribe to Nadine Menendez, is it about making the mortgage up to day
AUSA: Objection!
Judge: Ask again
Lustberg: Is this relevant to that?
Agent: I need to see the whole conversation.
Lustberg: Here she writes, Will is an as*shole

Lustberg: The lawyer asks Nadine, did you review the note I sent you, correct?
Agent: That's what it says.
Lustberg: It also says -
Judge: The jury will have this. There is no reason to ask it like this.
Lustberg: I want to know if he sees it.
Agent: I do.

Lustberg: Please enlarge this check, beneath the amount back - $23,500 - what does it say?
Agent: Loan auth. W. Hana to N.A.
Lustberg: You didn't testify about this on direct, did you?
Agent: I don't remember.

Judge: How much longer do you have?
Lustberg: 10 min

Lustberg: Look at these lines, that say "I know there will be a lot of hard work for all of us but hopefully it will come to fruition... Once I know your role, I will get your contract prepared." Do you know-
AUSA: Objection!
Judge: Sustained.

Judge: Wrap it up, sir.
Lustberg: Just a couple more things... I just need a few more moments. I'm going more slowly. You were asked questions if there was more money than the $30,000
Judge: Sustained!
Lustberg: Do you see where Nadine asks Mr. Daibes $36K?
Yes

Lustberg: One last on this subject. Line 956 on page 70, please... A voicemail from Nadine to Mr. Daibes, it says, "do me the favor of talking to Will, he wants me in the

office 8 hours a day, uh, thank you Fred."
Agent: I don't remember it specifically

Lustberg: Line 462 to 465, page 37 - the WhatsApp from Mr. Hana to Akmed Ahbed al Kareem
Agent: I don't recall specifics.
Lustberg: Ahmed Assam - who was he?
Agent: At this moment I don't recall.
Judge: Asked and answered. Next.
Lustberg: Hana and Shawky? Helmi?

Lustberg: Mr. Hana was involved in setting up meeting for Egyptian personnel in Washington?
Agent: I'd need to see.
Lustberg: Are these photographs of people in restaurants?
Agent: Yes.
Judge: Wrap it up.
Nothing further.
Counsel for Daibes: Just a few questions

Daibes' lawyer: The photos in the restaurants, Mr. Daibes is not in them, is he?
Agent: Not that I see.

Daibes' lawyer: You're new to the FBI Public Corruption unit, right?
Agent: Yes. I was on the health care squad.
Daibes' lawyer: And they picked you for this

Nothing further.
AUSA: The government calls Ted McKinney...
McKinney: I am the CEO for NASDA, National Assoc of State Departments of Agriculture. Previously at the Indiana Department of Agriculture to 2017. Then USDA, in foreign trade until 2021, Trump appointee

AUSA: Your job was to promote US exports - what % of US agricultural exports were to Egypt?
McKinney: Small but important - we had 60% of the market share of beef livers. Often those offals like liver and tongue are the key profit center for the rancher

McKinney: I went to the annual Dubai food show. I'd go to the office of the GCC. In late April 2019 we learned that Egypt had delisted

a number of halal certifiers in the US, and was making a monopoly for IS EG.
AUSA: How did you learn it?
McKinney: An email.

McKinney: We swung into action. We called the Egyptian ambassador in DC. When they moved to monopoly, on only one week's notice, prices went up.
Judge: Tell me about your history?
McKinney: My family raised pork in Indiana.
Judge: You were tuned in at age 17?
Yes

McKinney: My chief of staff told me Senator Menendez would be calling me on my cell phone. He did. He referenced a news article; he said Quit interfering with my constituent. I wanted to explain why - I was interrupted and the call ended shortly thereafter

AUSA: What was Senator Menendez' tone and demeanor?
McKinney: Serious to very serious. He was insisting, Stop! Stop interfering!
AUSA: Did any other member of Congress

interrupt you like that?
McKinney: No, never.

Judge Stein: We'll break here.

Chapter 15: Short Eyes of Union City

That time I flew with the eye doctor
To the Dominican
I wasn't being short eyes
Only saving taxpayer money

Why a new bottle for each cut eye?
Yeah I asked Harkin
Didn't he shake my hand at trial?
Didn't not only Cory but Lindsay Graham come?

This time I am alone
No Cory, Fetterman fucking me
Well fuck them, I say

Only Union City Cuban support me
And they're down to four percent
And even of them, only some
They'll chisel my name
Off the public school

Cutting like the cut eyes
Blind to history.

Chapter 16: Menendez Trial Day June 5, 2024

OK - now US v. Menendez, Judge Stein just said "full day of testimony"

All rise!
Judge Stein: Government, call your next witness.
FBI Agent Rachel Graves.
Assistant US Attorney: Did you prepare this summary chart?
Graves: Yes. But I didn't choose the underlying documents.
AUSA: Emails & texts - how many?
Graves: 1000s of pages

AUSA: Mr. Richenthal, please put up GX 1306.
[E&K Trucking, including its Chase Bank signature card]
AUSA: Special Agent Graves, what's the third name?
Graves: Elvis Parra, President.

AUSA: And this?
Graves: "Elvis Parra Indicted."

AUSA: Special Agent Graves, what is this?
Graves: Parts of a grand jury testimony...
AUSA: Play the audio
[Nadine voice mail to Hana, then Jose Uribe's email about a Sen Menendez cocktail fundraiser, "no podemos fallar" - we cannot fail.]

AUSA: Play the audio of December 13, 2018 [Nadine to Bob Menendez / "Ro Sorce" after car crash, "I'm going to call Progressive." Next up: the red Mercedes...]

AUSA: What did Nadine text to Hana?
Graves: I am so excited to be getting the car next week.
AUSA: What did Hana text Daibes?
Grave: Hey Fred can you please help Nadine with the car? Then here's Hernandez to Uribe: Cunningham is the lawyer

AUSA: Who texts Nadine here?
Graves: Andy. He texts, Are you still up, I can call you. Nadine says, I'm up. Then Andy

calls her, 25 minutes, 35 seconds.
AUSA: The next day, who does Nadine call?
Graves: Andy, for 3 minutes. Then Menendez, 1 minute. Then Hana

AUSA: Nadine wrote to Uribe, I will find out what is going on. Then what?
Graves: Nadine texted Menendez, Mon amour.. It got cold out so we can do whatever you want. Heart [emoji]
AUSA: Uribe writes to Nadine, I hope we can get together, you me and Bob. Then what?

Graves: Nadine texts, I am five minutes ago. Then, I am here. Then Ray Catena [car dealership] Leon from there is in her contacts.
AUSA: Play the next audio.
[Nadine: I didn't hear from Leon. I will go with Bob and look at the cars, Saturday, thanks so much]

AUSA: What does Nadine text Menendez?
Graves: Both cars have brown interior. Which one do you prefer?
AUSA: What does Menendez text?
Graves: Like them both. Whichever you prefer.

[Menendez rests chin in his hand, watching this]

Judge Stein: We'll break here.

AUSA: What does Nadine text to Menendez?
Graves: Mon amour, can Mike drive me to Edison [Ray Catena Mercedes], he'll never have to drive me again.
AUSA: What does Menendez reply?
Grave: Mon amour, Mike will be with me in Manhattan. I will see if Mateo can do it

AUSA: What does Nadine write to Uribe?
Agent Graves: She sends the Mercedes Benz Financial Services invoice.
AUSA: And what does Uribe respond?
Graves: I send you later. Then he forwards it and says, I don't want anything with my name on it

[While Nadine's texts to Bob and Uribe are being shown to jury, this just in from Nadine's new lawyer: US consents to her not being physically present at her June 12 hearing

AUSA: What does Nadine write here?
Agent Graves: Bob had to go down to Texas with some other Senators, about the border. Bob says it would have been easy if we had wrapped it all together.
AUSA: Page 50, line 965, August 5, 2019
Graves: Uribe says they'll meet

Judge Stein: We'll break

Cross examination.
Menendez' lawyer Adam Fee: So in this one Nadine said, I had to get my nails done - & that Nadine was renting a car for herself. It says Yes you can, not thank you, right?
Agent Graves: It says Yes you can.
Fee: How far down is thank you?
A: I don't know.

Judge Stein: We break here for the day.

Chapter 17: Uribe and Jersey All the Way Back

In the trial, cooperator Jose Uribe testified about holding a fundraiser for Menendez, mostly of Latinos truckers he said, as a precursor to getting Menendez to intervene and try to stop the case against him and his daughter Ana.

As Kurt dug deeper into Jersey and Menendez, the name Arnaldo Monzon came up, a man who had funded Omega 7 - Menendez had contributed to a legal defense fund - and who had shepherded Menendez from Union City politics to the Senate.

Along the way, it was said, Menendez had turned on his mentor William Musto and helped put him in jail. Now on his case to the black car with Jersey plate, Menendez derided Uribe the cooperator. But Menendez had been a cooperator himself. And a funder of terrorism, or at least the legal defense of accused terrorists.

Kurt would dig deeper into Jersey...

Chapter 18: Big Bob One and Two

Big Bob 1

I haunted the bars of Edgewater
Whenever not in session
This Persian carpet ice queen
Who knew she had gold bars in the bed?

Sure I could unfreeze weapons for tyrants
But every man has his needs, you know
A little baksheesh but it ain't over
You can keep my seat warm
But it's mine]

Bob 2

I beat the rap
They couldn't prove it.
And even though close
The people sent me back

So yeah I sicced Capitol Police
On Nadine's bullshit boyfriend
Fat man with a blonde companion
A dealer in Persian carpets

I'll help the halal beef liver monopoly mafia
I'm Big Bob

Chapter 19: Menendez Trial Day June 6, 2024

OK- US v Menendez trial continues, cross of FBI Agent, then Gurbir Grewal?

Menendez' lawyer Fee: In your work on this chart, regarding Nadine's former boyfriend Doug Anton-
Objection!
Sustained.
Fee: After the accident, Nadine's first call was not to Senator Menendez, correct?
Agent Grade: It was not.
Fee: Who is Gurbir Grewal?
A: NJ AG.

Menendez's lawyer Fee: Did you see anything about Senator Menendez called AG Grewal about a discriminatory prosecution-
Objection!
Sustained!
Fee: Did you see why he called Grewal?
Agent: I did not.

Fee: Did Menendez contact judges?
A: I need to look at the chart

Menendez's lawyer Fee: Did you see any messages in which Nadine told Senator Menendez about credit card problems?
Agent: I do not recall
Judge: Meaning, you have no idea.
Agent: Right.
Fee: You agree in row 336 Hana asks Nadine for nail salon address?
A: Can't say

Menendez' lawyer Fee: Here, Nadine tells Senator Menendez that an Uber is picking her up, not Mr. Hana's driver. She was lying, right?
Judge: Sustained!
Fee: Did you see Nadine asking Senator Menendez for financial assistance?
Agent: I didn't see any specifics

Menendez' lawyer Fee: I could take a break here, Your Honor.
Judge Stein: How much longer do you have?
Fee: An hour.
Judge: Keep going.

Fee: Do you remember payments at JPMorgan Chase by Nadine and why?
A: I don't know.

Menendez's lawyer Fee: Do you see here Nadine telling Hana "my ex is not paying me"?
Agent: I see that.
Fee: Did you see Nadine trying to get Hana to hire her ex boyfriend Doug Anton?
Agent: I don't recall.

Judge Stein: We'll break.

OK- now former NJ AG Gurbir Grewal, direct examination
AUSA Richenthal: What did Senator Menendez ask you to do?
Grewal: I asked him if it was about a pending criminal matter. He said yes.
Judge: Was there any discussion of how Hispanics were treated?
A: Yes

Grewal: I could tell you what I took him to mean

Judge: No, just want he said.
AUSA: Was he complaining?
Grewal: Complaining.
AUSA: How did he respond when you said you couldn't discuss it?
Grewal: Calmly, he moved to small talk

AUSA: Did you speak to the case prosecutors?
Grewal: Never. I wanted to insulate them. I'm not going to circumvent the process.
AUSA: What concern did you have if people learned that the senior senator raised a case to you?
Grewal: I didn't want it to chill them

Judge: Move on.
AUSA: No further questions.
Judge: Cross examination.
Menendez's lawyer Avi Weitzman: You were not a Federal employee at them time, right?
Grewal: I was not.
Weitzman: Your office did not get funding from the US Senate, did it?
Grewal: Not directly

Menendez's lawyer: Your Office had a duty to increase trust between immigrant communities and law enforcement, right?
Grewal: Yes.
Menendez's lawyer: Did Senator Menendez use the phrase "selective prosecution"?
Grewal: I don't remember him using that phrase

Menendez's lawyer: You're a former federal prosecutor - in 2 districts, right?
Grewal: I am...
Judge: Let's break.

Cross examination continues.
Menendez's lawyer: Do you recall telling the FBI you were not afraid of retribution from Senator Menendez?
Grewal: I was not afraid of retribution. I just didn't want to be on the bad side of an ally of the governor.

Menendez's lawyer: Didn't Dick Codey raise to you the case of Kevin Bannon, the basketball coach?
Grewal: I told him I wouldn't hear about that.

Menendez's lawyer: And he retaliated against you?
Grewal: A law that I couldn't run for governor.

Menendez's lawyer: Fair to say Dick Codey didn't know your practice?
AUSA: Objection to when he knew.
Judge: Sustained.
Menendez's lawyer: You are aware Senator Menendez acted to protect LGTBQ youth?
Grewal: I don't remember that

Menendez's lawyer: You reach out to Senator Menendez about your SEC position?
Grewal: I reached out to elected officials to tell them I was moving
Judge: Why, if you were a state official?
Grewal: I would be moving to DC
Menendez' lawyer: No further questions

Re-direct
AUSA Richenthal: About Dick Codey, do two wrongs make a right?
Objection! Sustained. Day over

Chapter 20: From Uribe to Grewal

Uribe

I should have known that trucker
Would be a motherfucker
Worse was insurance man
Wobbly like this diner *flan*

They found and filmed me scarfing fries
Nadine's say every fry eater dies

Grewal

I never even used the name
When I met with Gurbir Grewal
Now he sits here
Quoting his deputy calling me gross
Well I'll tell Telemundo
Andy Kim my ass
It's my seat

Chapter 21: Menendez Trial Day June 7, 2024

OK - now US v. Menendez, starting an hour late - will cooperator Uribe be today, after fingerprint expert?

Assistant US Attorney: Did a verifier ever disagree with a print that you verified?
Agent: Once. In 2011. The verifier said it was an exclusion.
AUSA: Were you given more training after that?
Agent: Yes.
AUSA: How many latent prints have you analyzed?
A: 1000s

AUSA: What was your involvement in this case?
Agent: Only latent print analysis.
AUSA: What is a known print?
Agent: Typically with a scanner or ink. We compare them to latent prints.

AUSA: Did you test gold coins?
Agent: Yes. But coins are not good for prints.

AUSA: Did you test gold bars?
Agent: Yes. But they were dinged up. And cash, it's like fabric. Money is fairly dirty, folded up in a wallet - not a good surface for a latent print. An envelope is better. We use "Undo" to remove the tape

AUSA: Put up GX 54-1-1, a piece of tape, correct?
Agent: Yes.... We place the latent print and the known print side by side.
AUSA: What do you look for?
Agent: Similarities or differences. Here, the ridge flow is similar...

[Amid this methodical testimony, here are US v. Menendez exhibit, cash and FRI lab memo

AUSA: Please zoom in on the manila envelope. What did you identify here?
Agent: The fingerprint of Robert Menendez. The left index finger...

[Last questions on cross of fingerprint expert]
Menendez's lawyer Fee: Does it look to you like this money was sitting somewhere a long time?
Objection! Sustained.
Fee: For the FBI, it is your duty to tell the truth?
Sustained! Sit down, Mr. Fee. Next witness...

Jose Uribe.
AUSA: Have you pled guilty to federal crimes?
Uribe: Yes. To bribing a Senator.
AUSA: Through who?
Uribe: His wife Nadine.
AUSA: Did you do it with others?
Uribe: With others. There - can I stand? - Will Hana.
Judge: Witness has IDed Mr. Hana

Uribe: I agree with Nadine to provide a car to Nadine to get the power and influence of Senator Menendez, for positive resolution for a colleague, and to stop and kill investigations
AUSA: Where did you grow up?

Uribe: Dominican Republic. I came here at 18

AUSA: Where did you move?
Uribe: Union City, New Jersey.
AUSA: Are you a US citizen?
Uribe: I became one in 1991. I went to Hudson County Community College, and worked in a factory.
AUSA: Then what?
Uribe: An insurance agency in Union City.

AUSA: How did you start there?
Uribe: I was insuring my used car and saw the place was busy so I asked to work there. The first month, he didn't pay me.
Judge: Why did you work for free?
Uribe: I fell in love with the business. Later I got my license.

Uribe: I lost my license, then formed Phoenix Risk Management. There, my son Omar was the license holder. I was the adviser and general manager.
AUSA: Who ran it?
Uribe: I did....
AUSA: Did you have to leave the insurance

business under cooperation agreement?
Yes

AUSA: Who was being investigated?
Uribe: Elvis Parra of E&K Trucking. And the driver Bienvenido Hernandez, who ran Prestige Trucking Express. I consider them almost brothers.
AUSA: What was the criminal investigation?
Uribe: Parra pled guilty and got probation

AUSA: How did you become aware of the investigation?
Uribe: Subpoena. Then Detective Lopez, she went to my daughter's house on a Saturday, very unpleasant, and out to Seattle to speak with my son Omar in the middle of a law school class

AUSA: Did you get worried?
Uribe: As a father you don't want your children faced with an investigation like this.... I talked to Will Hana at Andy Arslanian's office about it. He said for $250,000 he could make it go away. Through Nadine and Senator Menendez

AUSA: Did you tell anyone?
Uribe: I told Bien[venido] that my brother Will said he has a way to get a good resolution for Elvis' sentencing and the investigation, we should listen to him-
Judge: Who?
Uribe: Will Hana. We met at a Marriott in Teaneck.

Uribe: At the meeting Will mentioned Nadine.
AUSA: How did Bien and Elvis Parra react?
Uribe: Positively. That if Elvis got no jail time and the investigations were killed they would pay.

Judge Stein. Let's break.

They've back.
AUSA: Did you do a fundraiser for Senator Menendez?
Uribe: I did. In a private room in Villa Amalfi in Cliffside Park on July 13, 2018.
AUSA: Did Bob Menendez attend?
Uribe: Yes. He said he was impressed by the business people I brought

AUSA: How much did you raise for Senator Menendez at the fundraiser?
Uribe: $50,000 - I gave $5000 myself. We had an afterparty. Nadine, Will, Mr. Menendez...
AUSA: Then what?
Uribe: Detective Lopez visited my daughter. I was, I hate to repeat the word, fucked.

Uribe: Then at another restaurant in New Jersey, we met: Nadine, Will, Senator Menendez and myself.
AUSA: How would you describe Mr. Hana's behavior with Menendez?
Uribe: It seemed like he wanted to suck up to Senator Menendez...

AUSA: Then what?
Uribe: Nadine complained to me, the men in her life never come through, that Will didn't get her the car he promised.
AUSA: What did you say?
Uribe: I said I would provide a car as soon as she helps me. She acknowledged knowing part of the deal

Uribe: Nadine said she know about E&K Trucking.
AUSA: Why did you want to do a deal for a car?
Uribe: To protect my family. I told her, I will stand by my word, as long as she delivers on her promise.
AUSA: What did you write to Bien?
Uribe: I received good news

Judge: We'll break for the week.

Chapter 22: Voice of Uribe

I too like the Mercedes Benz
Parking in Italian restaurant
Parking lots with bricks of cash
But I never heard of gold

Wael, my brother, he didn't follow through
Elvis, Bienvenido and me
We had to do it on our own
Plying this Lebanese *hermana*
with car payments
To the reach the sweater-vested

Short eyes
I ain't going to jail for him.

Chapter 23: Trial Day June 10, 2024

OK - now US v. Menendez, cooperator Uribe still on direct, describing $15,000 in cash to Nadine for Bob to end NJ probe that could implicate his daughter

Assistant US Attorney: What did you write to Nadine?
Uribe: I have to meet with you. I am worried, nothing is happening.
AUSA: What did you mean by that?
Uribe: The investigation was not being stopped, nor on the case of Elvis Parra. I wrote, Please get your car

Uribe: Will [Hana] is the one who promised her a car, but I am the one who provided it.
AUSA: What did you write?
Uribe: LOL, Lord Oh Lord, go get your car.
AUSA: What did she write?
Uribe: That Leo at Ray Catena [Mercedes dealer] said the car was sold

AUSA: What were you asking for?
Uribe: I asked Bien[venido] Hernandez [of Prestige Trucking] for $15,000, since Will hadn't paid.
AUSA: Did Bien give you $15,000 in cash?
Uribe: No.
AUSA: Did you tell Will about the $15,000?
Uribe: Yes.
AUSA: Here's lines 19-20

AUSA: Nadine texts you, You make dreams come true, I will always remember that. When do you think she meant?
Uribe: She will comply with her part of the deal, hopefully.
AUSA: Then what?
Uribe: She wrote, we'll all have a great 2019. Meaning, she'll comply

Uribe: Then Nadine was trying to set up my meeting with Senator Menendez, over cigars and a drink. I said, he probably have a thousand things to do, we can pick another day.
AUSA: Why did you write that?
Uribe: I didn't want her to feel no pressure

Uribe: I wrote, Thank our friend.
AUSA: Meaning who?
Uribe: Senator Menendez.
AUSA: Here Nadine texted you about "Part 2" - what do you think she meant?
Uribe: The investigation into Bien Hernandez.
AUSA: Where did you meet?
Uribe: Sophia's restaurant in NJ

AUSA: Did Nadine complaint to you about Hana not delivering on anything else but the car?
Uribe: That he didn't give her a job at his meat company.
AUSA: What did Will tell you if anyone was going to help with his meat business?
Uribe: Nadine and Senator Menendez.

AUSA: Did Nadine help you about Will not helping with mortgage payments?
Uribe: Yes. She was about to lose her home. She was very worried. She asked me to tell Wael to pay her mortgage by Monday morning....

AUSA: Here what did Nadine write to you?
Uribe: That she wanted to meet to get information to resolve Part 2, that "this stands always, not only Part 2 but for a lifetime, I will not forget what a true friend you are." She will be there for me.

AUSA: Did Will complain to you about Nadine?
Uribe: Yes. That she only cares about money.
Judge: Let's break.

They've back
AUSA: Did you find that Elvis and Bien paid Will?
Uribe: Yes. I was angry - I had set up the deal.
AUSA: What did Will tell you about getting $125,000 from them?
Uribe: He confirmed it, at Ventanas Restaurant. Will wanted to set up a trucking company

Uribe: There was a brick of cash, $25,000. I told Will, I'm going to take it, I'm paying for Nadine's car. He said, Take it brother.

AUSA: Then what?
Uribe: Detective Lopez wanted to interview Ana. I reached out to Nadine immediately, for her to tell the Senator

Uribe: Nadine told me that the Senator told her, It would have been so so easy if we had wrapped both together.
AUSA: What did you understand by that?
Uribe: If the Senator had knowledge of Part 1 and Part 2 from the very beginning, just like Elvis got probation

AUSA: Did you have an understanding if Senator Menendez had done anything on behalf of Elvis?
Menendez' lawyer: Objection! Lack of foundation.
Judge: Sustained.
AUSA: He didn't ask you questions about who Elvis Parra or E&K Trucking was, correct?
Uribe: Correct.

AUSA: What did you explain to him?
Uribe: That I was worried that the authorities were handling an investigation that could

reach to my daughter. I asked, Don't let these people hurt my daughter.
AUSA: What did Robert Menendez say?
Uribe: He would look into it

AUSA: Who paid for the dinner?
Uribe: I did.
AUSA: What was your understanding of the status?
Uribe: Elvis got a good resolution and I was close to getting peace for my family.
AUSA: Did you tell Robert Menendez you were paying for Nadine car?
Uribe: No. He knew

Menendez's lawyer: Objection!
Judge (to Uribe) Why did you think Mr. Menendez knew?
Uribe: They kept trying to set up by the meeting with me, the only reason was payments I was making.
AUSA: Did Nadine ever tell you what to say and not say to Menendez?
Uribe: No

Uribe: I texted Fernando, "el primo got a call about a late payment." I mistyped it,

masculine, primo.
Judge: If you wrote el prima it would be right?
Uribe: La prima, it should have been. I told Fernando to pay with my card from Frank & Sons Logistics.

Judge: Ok, let's break

Back.
AUSA: Who paid the bill at Segovia's restaurant with Senator Menendez, Nadine and her daughter?
Uribe: I did.
AUSA: These text messages, directing your attention to Row 3, can you read it, August 8, 2020?
Uribe: Segovia is very private, I would love to meet

AUSA: Here, Nadine texts you, Are you free for dinner - what did you say?
Uribe: That I am busy, but open. She said Bob made a reservation 7:30. I said, On my way.
AUSA: And this?

Uribe: Nadine says Sabine thanks her tip - she meant tio, uncle, I am her uncle.

AUSA: When did you become aware of a Federal investigation involving you?
Uribe: 2022 - the FBI took my cell phone, subpoenaed me to grand jury.
AUSA: Publish GX 11e1, the subpoena, June 16, 2022, for all records about payments to Senator or Nadine Menendez

AUSA: What next?
Uribe: Nadine wanted to meet with me. We met at the Glenpointe Marriott. I told her, They went to my house, gave me a bunch of subpoenas. She said, Hermano, I get sick every time I look at papers. She said she lost her cell phone at Grand Central

Uribe: She asked me how I would explain paying for her car.
AUSA: What did you say?
Uribe: That I'd say she was a friend and that I help until she could pay me back.
AUSA: Had you ever discussed it as a loan?
Uribe: Never.

AUSA: Was it a loan?
Uribe: It was not

Judge Stein: We'll break here

They've back:
AUSA: Between the FBI subpoena-ing you and your indictment in September 2023, did you meet with prosecutors?
Uribe: Once. About my failure to file taxes.
AUSA: Did you decide to cooperate?
Uribe: No.

AUSA: Later did you decide to cooperate?
Uribe: Yes, hoping to get a better sentence.
AUSA: How many times have we met with prosecutors?
Uribe: 10 to 15 times. FBI was there sometimes too.
AUSA: Did you plead guilty?
Uribe: Yes, under a cooperation agreement.

Uribe: I pled guilty to using a fake tax return to get a loan from Santander bank, too. Also an SBA loan....
AUSA: With the other crimes, what is the maximum sentence you could receive?

Uribe: 95 years. I am hoping for no incarceration.

AUSA: What do you have to do?
Uribe: Tell the truth.
AUSA: No further questions.
Cross examination.
Hana's lawyer: In your allocution did you state anything about a cash payment to Mr. Hana?
Uribe: I cannot answer yes or no as Mr. Hana is part for the deal

Hana's lawyer: You didn't have any details, right?
Uribe: Not step by step.
Hana's lawyer: So you didn't deal with Hana, you went to Nadine, right?
Uribe: I can't say the timing.
Hana's lawyer: You lost hope in Will, right?
Uribe: Correct.

Hana's lawyer: I could break here.
Judge: Let's break, then.

Chapter 24: Beef Liver Strategy

Was it start to have Hana's counsel, and not Menendez', start the cross of Uribe, at day's end? By the end of the trial, will the flavor left in jurors' mouths at the end of this day matter? In Menendez' earlier mistrial, one juror was ready to convict on Count 18 then thought better? Here? After the jury left, the defense said they have a witness who goes out of town June 17, can he testify out of order? It seems unlikely.

Chapter 25: Trial Day June 11, 2024

OK - now in US v Menendez, cooperator Uribe on (1st) cross examination, by Wael "Beef Liver" Hana's lawyer. Next up is Menendez' lawyer

Hana's lawyer: Isn't it true you didn't mention Mr. Hana mentioned Senator Menendez until many meetings into your cooperation with the government?
Uribe: I don't have a recollection.
Hana's lawyer: At the bar, there was no discussion with Hana about Part 1 & 2?
No

Hana's lawyer: Are you aware that Nadine referred Doug Anton to Hana as a possible lawyer for Elvis Parra, for $20,000 for probation, or $150,000 if it went to trial?
Uribe: I had no knowledge.
Hana's lawyer: Fair to say you lie a lot?
Uribe: I have lied

Hana's lawyer: You ripped off the SBA?
Uribe: I used the wrong numbers.
Hana's lawyer: Fake numbers, right?
Uribe: To get the loan.
Hana's lawyer: You are testifying to get a lower sentence, right?
Uribe: Less than 95 years, I am hoping. Maybe no jail

Judge Stein: Let's break.
[With jury out of room]
Hana's lawyer Lustberg: We want to cross him about a car crash and most about his failure to pay child support, given his claims of being a family man. He says the woman he didn't pay got into another relationship

AUSA Richenthal: We don't want to put into the public record things we want out of it... What Mr. Lustberg just said is inaccurate, I'm not saying intentionally so. This is deeply personal.
Judge Stein: We're dancing around some things here

Judge Stein: What about the strip clubs?
AUSA Richenthal: I'd ask Your Honor to be

carefully how to describe the conduct -
Lustberg: I will too, it's in the papers, he's claimed to be a choirboy but this goes directly to morality.
Judge: You have a lot on him

Judge: The strip club, essentially irrelevant. The child support, on a 403 weighing, I'm going to exclude it too. It doesn't go to truthfulness. You've got so much to work with on the cross. So this falls into 403. It's prejudicial.

Judge: OK, now we'll break.

Cross continues, by Hana's lawyer
Hana's lawyer: After the prosecutors told you that you were the target of a tax investigation, you pled guilty saying you bribed Senator Menendez, right?
Uribe: After I pled guilty I had to tell the truth.

[After lunch break declared by Judge Stein, Hana's lawyer is still at it]
Hana's lawyer: You can't even remember how

many frauds you've committed, do you?
Uribe: I pled to insurance fraud and theft by deception
Hana's lawyers: You stole insurance premiums
No.

Judge Stein: OK, Mr. Fee, try to avoid objections.
Menendez' lawyer Fee: Read that, Mr. Uribe, and let me know when you're finished.
Uribe: OK.
Fee: Ana was not in touch with your daughter Vanessa when she called you and said, I'm pregnant and I need a job.
Yes.

Menendez's lawyer Fee: So you put her as head of the company you were illegally running?
Uribe: Can I add to your question?
Fee: No. Your son refused to run it -
Uribe: He went to Seattle... I use my family to have the opportunity to share my business, we share

Menendez's lawyer Fee: You used your nephew at Santander to commit wire fraud?
Uribe: He was a salesman there
Fee: Santander is an international bank, right?
Uribe: I know it operates in the US.
Fee: And you defrauded the SBA?
Uribe: I used a fake tax return, yes

Menendez's lawyer Fee: You remember Jose Suero & Hoboken 1st Class Corp - and taking premiums from them for three and a half years, right?
Uribe: Yes
Fee: Then one of his limos got into an accident, right?
Uribe: I don't remember.
Fee: Suero closed?
A: He's in NJ

Menendez's lawyer Fee: After you got Nadine the car, she stopped answering you as quickly, right?
Uribe: Yes.
Fee: You felt she was using you?
Uribe: I never thought that.
Fee: You never talked about the car with

Senator Menendez?
Uribe: I did not.

Menendez's lawyer Fee: Nadine never told you that she told Senator Menendez you paid for her car, did she?
Uribe: She did not.
Fee: You know Senator Menendez is an advocate for Latinos?
Uribe: I do not follow Mr. Menendez, what he likes about his job.

Judge: We'll break here.

They've back
Menendez's lawyer Fee: You hosted a fundraiser for Senator Menendez, with nearly all Latino truckers?
Uribe: Yes.
Fee: And Senator Menendez asked the attendees to share with him their stories of any problems?
Uribe: I don't remember that

Menendez's lawyer Fee: Here, his [then] staffer Samantha Maltzman texted you a story

about Latino museum opening in DC after work by Senator Menendez?
Uribe: I see that.

Menendez's lawyer Fee: You never told Senator Menendez that you were operating without a license, did you?
Uribe: I don't recall telling him that.
Fee: Andy told you Doug Anton was crazy in love with Nadine?
Uribe: Yes
Judge: That's not for the truth, jurors

Menendez's lawyer Fee: You claim the Senator called you from his office in DC and said That thing that you asked me, there is nothing there, you have your peace?
Uribe: Yes.
Fee: He didn't ask for a bribe, right?
Uribe: No he did not.

Judge: We'll stop for the day here.

Chapter 26: Strip Club and Short Eyes Out

While some consider it salacious, this excluded so-called strip club issue, to others it seems that a cooperating witness opens himself up to all questions. Still others point to the dangling claims of underage prostitutes in the DR in Menendez's last trial - or where those promoted by Cuba? Gwendolyn Beck, Menendez' girlfriend at the time, and Epstein victim Virginia Guiffre?

Chapter 27: Menendez Trial Day June 12, 2024

OK - now in US v Menendez, cooperator Uribe still on cross examination, with "strip club issue" excluded -

Jury has still not been brought it.
Judge Stein: I got the midnight submission from Menendez [Inner City Press tweeted a

screenshot of it, just after it went in, bid to impeach Hana] and I disagree with it. But I am asking the parties, stop with midnight filings

Judge Stein: Bring in the jury... You have my decision... Jury entering!
[Jurors enter]
Judge Stein: Mr. Fee, you may continue and conclude your cross examination.
Menendez's lawyer Fee: You texted Nadine, You don't love me anymore, correct?
Uribe: It was a joke

Menendez's lawyer Fee: The meeting on the backyard patio, didn't you say "We are working people," about Bien Hernandez?
Uribe: We were talking, drinking Grand Marnier.
Fee: You spelled out the deal to Nadine - not to Sen Menendez?
Uribe: I talked elements with him

Menendez's lawyer Fee: You claim you wrote down the names for Senator Menendez in Sept 2019 - but why, if Nadine had them?
AUSA: Objection!

Judge: Sustained.
Fee: Here's the patio where you met Senator Menendez?
Uribe: It was dark.

Menendez's lawyer Fee: You say Senator Menendez rang a little bell & said, "mon amour, bring paper"?
Uribe: The piece of paper was brought into the backyard by Mrs. Menendez, where I wrote the names.
Fee: So there are gaps in your memory?
Uribe: I give substance

Menendez's lawyer Fee: The little bell that you say Senator Menendez rang was it bigger than my fist?
Judge: Sustained! Lower your voice! You're saying the size of the bell is important?
Fee: I am
Judge: Was there anyone else on the patio?
Uribe: Just Senator & me

Menendez's lawyer Fee: Senator Menendez did not promise any particular outcome?
Uribe: The word promise was not used...
Fee: How much did you spend at the

Glenpointe Marriott bar from 2018 to 2020?
Uribe: I don't know.
Fee: Did you drive drunk?
Objection!

Menendez's lawyer Fee: You were using Xanax?
Uribe: Sometimes when I have a stomach...
Fee: You had no prescription but got it from family?
Uribe: Yes.
Fee: You were stressed out.
Uribe: Yes.
Fee: When you met Sen Menendez you were drinking?
Uribe: Sometimes

Menendez's lawyer Fee: After the backyard meeting, Senator Menendez told you to watch out, there were many police around, you should not be drinking and driving?
Uribe: We had Grand Marnier.
Fee: You only brought up Prestige [Trucking] after you drank?
Uribe: Yes

Menendez's lawyer Fee: After the backyard meeting, Senator Menendez told you to watch out, there were many police around, you should not be drinking and driving?
Uribe: We had Grand Marnier.
Fee: You only brought up Prestige [Trucking] after you drank?
Uribe: Yes

Menendez's lawyer Fee: What is the impact on your memory when you use Xanax and alcohol?
AUSA: Objection!
Judge: When did you take Xanax?
Uribe: In the morning.
Fee: The senator told you he saved your ass - you say he used the word "culito"?
Uribe: Yes.

Menendez's lawyer Fee: You pled guilty to tax evasion. Why?
Uribe: Because I was guilty.
Fee: You understand the prosecutors were focused on Senator Menendez?
Uribe: I was investigated for the car to Nadine Menendez

Menendez's lawyer Fee: The patio, the Segovia's meeting - did the prosecutors question those?
Objection! Sustained.
Fee: Is you goal here to do anything to protect yourself and your family?
AUSA: Objection!
Judge: Sustained.
Fee: Nothing further

Jury out
Judge: Mr. Fee, after a few more years at Paul Hastings you too many have a little bell. We'll break.

They're back.
AUSA: Did this text reflect Nadine telling Senator Menendez she was looking for the right bell, 5 days before the backyard meeting with Mr. Uribe?
Witness: It does.
Menendez's lawyer Fee: Are you aware of Nadine's collection of bells that don't ring?

Next witness is from the Bureau of Engraving and Printing.
Witness: The Federal Reserve Board tells us how many bills they wanted printed in a particular year.
AUSA: Show GX HL1-4. Are all bills now Next Gen?
Witness: All but the ones and the twos.

[While waiting for judge and jury to come back, Menendez is sitting or leaning back against the defense table, chatting with his lawyer Adam Fee. Daibes is leaning back in the back row. Prosecutors knock a water bottle on the floor]
All rise!

Next witness is US Attorney for the District of NJ Philip R. Sellinger.
Assistant [SDNY] US Attorney: Who selects the US Attorney?
Sellinger: The Senators recommend to the President.
Judge: The President of the US?
Sellinger: Yes.

AUSA: When did you meet Senator Menendez?

Sellinger: All the way back to 2000. Later we golfed, with our sons. And dinner with my wife, and he with Nadine.

AUSA: How many people went to their wedding?

Sellinger: 65 to 70.

AUSA: When did you begin speaking with Robert Menendez about becoming US Attorney?

Sellinger: In 2016 in the run up to the election between Hillary Clinton and Donald Trump. At Senator Menendez' recommendation I spoke with Senator Booker

Sellinger: Hillary Clinton was not elected, so the discussions of my becoming US Attorney came to an end.

AUSA: What about 2020?

Sellinger: Joseph Biden was elected President. I expressed an interest again, to Senator Menendez. We met one on one at his office

Sellinger: It was Dec 15, 2020. I flew Tampa to BWI, then Dulles to Sarasota.
AUSA: Was the meeting in your calendar?
Sellinger: No. I thought it might be disruptive at my firm, Greenberg Traurig; my secretaries had access to my calendar. So I did not list it

Sellinger: I talked about what I might to as US Attorney. Then Senator Menendez mentioned Fred Daibes, that he thought he was being treated unfairly. Senator Menendez said he hoped that if I became US Attorney I would look at it closely

AUSA: How did you respond?
Sellinger: I said that any case that came before me I would take a look at.
AUSA: How many cases does the Office have?
Sellinger: Approximately 1500.
AUSA: Had you heard of Fred Daibes?
Sellinger: Yes. In a lawsuit, him and his bank

AUSA: What was your understanding of Menendez' relationship with Fred Daibes?
Sellinger: I understood that they were friends.
AUSA: The lawsuit in which Mr. Daibes was

adverse, did Senator Menendez bring it up in 2020?
Sellinger: No.

AUSA: When you met with Senator Booker, did Senator Booker brought up any particular cases?
Sellinger: No.... On the Daibes case, I called Senator Menendez back and told him that I might have to recuse myself from any case involving Mr. Daibes.

AUSA: When Menendez told you he could not nominate you, what did he say?
Sellinger: That the White House wanted multiple candidates, something else. This was in late December.
AUSA: Who did he recommend?
Sellinger: Esther Suarez

Sellinger: I told Senator Menendez I would still be interested. He said Ms. Suarez had a second White House interview. That was early April 2021.
AUSA: When did Robert Menendez tell you that you were being put forward,

recommended?
Sellinger: Early summer

AUSA: What was the process?
Sellinger: White House interview, FBI interview, interview by Democratic and Republican counsel for the Judiciary Committee.

AUSA: After you were sworn in, how many cases did you flag for possible recusal?
Sellinger: Four.

Sellinger: I was recused from the Daibes case and two others.
Judge: We'll break here

After robing room conference, Judge Stein emerges at 5:38 pm to say he has requested info from Nadine Menendez's doctors, has pushed her trial from July 8 to August 5, should have medical info by then, he says.

Chapter 28: Full Circle, William Musto

On his way out of the courthouse, Menendez said (in Spanish) that he didn't asking anything inappropriate of Sellinger. Now reading his history, Inner City Press thought to ask him about when he testified against his mentor, William Musto

Chapter 29: Trial Interruptus June 13, 2024

Co-defendant Daibes has not come to trial, is awaiting his doctor in a hotel. Judge Stein says no trial today; jurors will be told they can go - and will be paid, he adds. Vlog (before that news) next, incl on US v. Guo, & UN

Jury entering
Judge Stein: It is unfortunate but there is nothing that can be done. Enjoy the day, it's good weather and you will get your per diem. See you tomorrow.
Jury exiting.
Hana's lawyer Lustberg: Don't allow in Hana's failure to register under FARA

Assistant US Attorney Richenthal: That we didn't charge Hana for failure to register under FARA, there's CIPA litigation...

Menendez's lawyer Fee: The Boston Red Sox first basement went to Congress about the Dominican Republic and didn't register under

FARA
[Some asking: is this a hypothetical, or true? Richard Gere has also been raised by the defense] #FARAfollies

Judge: You're making the argument that Hana is George Clooney?
[Insert self-deprecating joke; soft laughter from the gallery]
Judge: Apparently Menendez did check. Is Hana some third baseman?
Defense: There was nothing ominous about interacting with Mr. Hana

Menendez's lawyer Fee: We're going to argue there was no bribery for Senator Menendez to be an agent of Egypt. Hana and FARA, it's just a red herring.
AUSA Richenthal: There was a previous case, involving a former Congressman and Venezuela.

Hana's lawyer Lustberg: Citizens, non-citizens, they are permitted to be heard. Our position is that Mr. Hana was absolutely permitted to do what he was doing. It's allowed. Everyone doesn't need to register under FARA.

Judge: Enough for now.

And then the prosecutors were in the cafeteria and others better placed said what Daibes has isn't COVID, it's...

Inner City Press

www.ingramcontent.com/pod-product-compliance
Lightning Source LLC
Chambersburg PA
CBHW071514220526
45472CB00003B/1027